This production B-17C, one of thirty-eight, was assigned to the Materiel Division at Wright Field, Ohio, in late 1940 for preservice testing. Basically an improved B with revised armament positions, self-sealing tanks, and armor. Twenty of the Cs went to the RAF as Fortress Mk.Is while some of the others were reworked to D standards and saw action in the early weeks of the Pacific War. When the RAF took them into combat in July 1941 they proved vulnerable and not really combat ready. The AAF came to the same conclusion late in the year over the Pacific. *NASM Groenhoff Collection*

The first most drastic model change in the Flying Fortress came in September 1941 with the B-17E, as *Esmeralda* reveals during a factory test flight near Seattle. Armament was drastically improved with upper and lower power gun turrets and a tail gun position, armor was increased, and the tail was completely redesigned. This was the model which launched the Eighth Air Force's bombing campaign from England on 17 August 1942. *Boeing via Frederick A. Johnsen*

and success, let alone twice. During the 30th anniversary of the Air Corps from late July to early August 1939, B-17s broke several national and international records for speed, payload, and altitude.

In spite of such success, there were no orders for B-17s in 1938, an almost fatal mistake fully realized in 1941 when American airmen would be struggling not only to fight back but simply to survive. Once again Boeing barely survived through a few men who led a headline campaign to convince Congress and the public that the B-17 was worth having. From that point on, the Flying Fortress began to take its place in history, propelled in the public mind to a large extent by the prewar films *Test Pilot* with Clark Gable and *I Wanted Wings* with William Holden.

A single B-17A was converted from a Y-series airframe, then 39 B-17Bs, 38 B-17Cs, and 42 B-17Ds were ordered in succession; 119 aircraft, a very small beginning. The Y1B-17A was used as a test bed for the turbo supercharger, which would become standard on every model thereafter. This simple addition boosted the aircraft's service ceiling from 31,000 to

Redmond Annie, a B-17F, has just been serviced for a training mission over California as its crew arrives. Stateside training Forts became more than well-worn as the months went by. The balance between having an effective teaching tool and the needs of overseas combat theaters was a difficult one. No

Opposite page top, a B-17F heads out of Pueblo Army Air Field, Colorado, on a training mission in 1943. A combat crew was created slowly. First the individual members were trained at specialized bases, then sent to combat crew training fields where they were assembled into teams. The weeding out process was difficult...there were good crews and bad crews. After a number of training sorties flying together, the crew was either given a new aircraft to fly overseas or shipped out direct to the theater and a bomb group. *USAF via Stan Piet*

one envied those who had to make the decisions. Training aircraft were used to their last hour with stretched, sloppy control cables and tired engines. *USAF via Stan Piet*

Opposite page bottom, getting a thorough going over, *Hannah* is given new life for more training missions. Maintenance was a constant on every U.S. training field. The airplanes were worked hard as AAF leaders kept pushing the limits on how many men could be trained in a brief space of time. By 1943, experiments were made in shortening the time required to train crewmen, and the results were surprisingly good. Quality did not suffer, and more men were available for combat. *USAF via Stan Piet*

A fuel truck pulls up to a B-17F in Florida for yet another training mission. Fortunately the Fort was easy to fly, even on two engines. Pilots and crews could be pushed hard and still perform well, a preview of what took place in combat. *USAF*

38,000ft, with top speed increased from 239mph at 5,000ft to 271mph at 25,000ft. Typical of Boeing's determination, the supercharger project was entirely company funded...the Army never paid a penny for this war winning capability even though it ordered all heavy bombers of any type to be so equipped from this point on.

The B-17B incorporated not only the turbos in a redesigned engine cowling and accessory section but a larger rudder, redesigned nose, fuel system improvements, and additional self-protecting armament, changed from .30cal to .50cal machine guns. Even more armament was added to the B-17C with flush teardrop shaped waist windows and a deepened ventral gun position. A football shaped ADF antenna fairing replaced the large loop under the nose as well. With the B-17D came engine cowl flaps, twin upper and lower gun mounts, more crew armor plate, self sealing fuel tanks, redesigned bomb racks and release equipment, a low pressure oxygen system, and a new 24 (vs. 12) volt electrical system.

With the B-17E came the definitive combat Fortress shape with its hallmark redesigned massive vertical fin and rudder. Armor and armament were increased due to hard earned combat lessons learned

The training Fortress line at Casper, Wyoming, March 1943, was always subject to the weather in the northern U.S., but poor conditions were never allowed to stop the process. After all, the combat groups flew in some of the worst weather imaginable, and crews would have to know how to deal with it. One of the deficiencies of early-war training was instrument flying. Not until mid-1943 did the AAF increase the amount of training in poor visual conditions. The results six months down the road were very evident, particularly in the European Theater.
Joe Manos

by the Royal Air Force (RAF) with their Fortress Is (B-17Cs). A top turret was added, along with a remote control belly turret (first 112 aircraft), then a manned ball turret, each with twin .50cal machine guns. The fuselage aft of the radio compartment was increased in diameter with square waist gun positions, leading to a new tail gunner's position with twin .50s. Windows were added to the top of the cockpit, and the side windows were enlarged for the pilots. Sockets for additional .50cals showed up in a number of places. A total of 512 B-17Es were built.

The B-17F brought with it full wartime mass production and the determination of the American worker to get the war over with. A total of 3,405 were built by Boeing, Lockheed-Vega, and Douglas. Over 400 changes were made to create this model of the Fort, from the clear Plexiglas nose and widened propeller blades to dozens of internal changes, including fuel tanks in the outer wing panels, called "Tokyo Tanks." Range was boosted to a phenomenal 4,220mi with a top speed of 325mph. Max-

A B-17F shares the ramp at Muroc AAB, California, with three Erco PQ-13 aerial targets, manned. In 1942, the PQ designation was assigned to powered targets which could also be flown by pilots, the most popular being the Culver PQ-14, based on the prewar Cadet. Supposedly only two PQ-13s were built from two Ercoupe 415C civil aircraft, but this photo proves that wrong. It seems every civil aircraft manufacturer tried to get the military to buy versions of their machines.
Via Frederick A. Johnsen

A line of new B-17Fs from all three manufacturers stretches across a ramp in the midwest. Though some pilots thought they could tell the differences between Boeing, Douglas, and Lockheed airframes, most said they couldn't tell any difference at all. Perceived differences had much to do with individual airframes than with manufacturers...some were fine handling, fast ships while others seemed to be dogs no matter who built them. Every airplane had its owns quirks and foibles.
George Ochs via EAA Library

Miss Barbara was one of the 305th Bomb Group's combat B-17Fs, flying out of Grafton Underwood in 1943. That year was the roughest as mission after mission faced fierce Luftwaffe opposition in the form of determined, talented fighter pilots and skilled flak gunners. Though AAF leadership believed bomber formations could defend themselves without long range fighter escort they were tragically wrong. *USAF*

The most famous B-17 of the them all, the *Memphis Belle*, on the ramp at National Airport during her post-combat 1943 war-bond tour. Though she wasn't really the first Eighth Air Force bomber to complete twenty-five missions, the AAF built its PR campaign around telling the public that it was. The attention was overwhelming at each stop as the crew got out to greet the public and encourage them to buy bonds. The bomber's fame increased enormously with the release of William Wyler's color documentary centered around the aircraft and its crew. *USAF*

imum bomb load was boosted to 9,600lbs.

The definitive combat Flying Fortress, the chin turreted B-17G, was built in larger numbers (8,680) than any other version. Beginning with the B-17G-50-BO, the waist positions were staggered to give each gunner more room to maneuver, and the windows could be completely enclosed to ward off the frigid air. A new tail turret, built at Cheyenne, Wyoming, was incorpo-rated on the final examples in addition to cheek gun positions on either side of the nose. When Hitler invaded Poland in 1939, the Army Air Corps had but twenty-three B-17s on strength, with another fifty-three added in 1940. From one Y1B-17 built every two weeks in 1937, Fortress produc-tion jumped to a peak of over sixteen per day in April 1944. By the time it was all over, 12,731 B-17s had been built.

✪ Fortress Under Siege ✪

The first combat mission flown by the Flying Fortress wasn't an American operation at all. RAF Bomber Command Lend-Lease B-17Cs attacked the German port of Wilhelmshaven on 8 July 1941, but subsequent missions left the British unimpressed, and their under-gunned, under-armored Fortresses were withdrawn from service. On 7 December 1941 there were twelve AAF B-17s at Hickam Field, and another twelve—from the 7th Bomb Group—were in the process of arriving from California.

Chief of the Army Air Forces Gen. Hap Arnold (right) and Under Secretary of War Robert Patterson pose with the crew of *Memphis Belle* at National Airport during their war bond tour. From left to right, back row, are S/Sgt. Cecil Scott, Capt. James A. Verinis, Patterson, Capt. Charles Leighton, Capt. Robert K. Morgan, Capt. Vincent Evans, Arnold, and T/Sgt. Robert J. Hanson. In the front row are S/Sgt. Casimer Nastal, S/Sgt. Clarence B. Winchell, T/Sgt. Harold P. Loch, and S/Sgt. John P. Quinlan.
USAF

The crew of *Patsy Ann* walks toward debriefing after a mission to Bordeaux in 1944. These are worn faces trying to bring up a smile for the camera. Combat in a bomber over Germany was brutal physically, mentally, and emotionally. The high-loss rates cracked even the best of men, but they kept on doing the job until it was over. *USAF*

By the end of the attack, four of the B-17s at Hickam and one of the 7th's Forts were destroyed. The rest of the B-17s were damaged, some worse than others.

At Clark Field near Manila, sixteen of thirty-five Forts were destroyed in the initial Japanese attacks. The 19th Bomb Group tried to retaliate by launching six B-17s on the first American bombing raid of the war—an unsuccessful antishipping mission—on 9 December 1941. The next day more missions were launched, and the legend of Capt. Colin P. Kelly, Jr. was made when he attacked and reported possibly sinking what he thought was a battleship. In reality it was a heavy cruiser which was only damaged. On the way back his B-17C was bounced by Zeros, one flown by Saburo Sakai, who would go on to become one of Japan's leading aces with sixty-four aerial victories.

With the Fort mortally wounded, Kelly ordered the crew to bail out but he did not make it. Though a ship was not sunk, Kelly was credited with destroying the battleship *Haruna* and recommended for the Medal of Honor. The mistake never took away from his selfless sacrifice in staying with the B-17 too long, allowing his crew to survive.

The first B-17E assigned to the Eighth Air Force arrived at Polebrook, England on 1 July 1942. The first mission was to bomb Rouen in occupied France. Gen. Ira C. Eaker—in his B-17 *Yankee Doodle*—led a group of twelve Forts from the 97th Bomb Group there on 17 August. In early November 1942, several groups of the Eighth's Forts were detached to North Africa following the Allied invasion, beginning a long history of B-17s in the Mediterranean in the Twelfth and Fifteenth Air Forces.

In mid 1942 the B-17F began to arrive in England, and by 1943 it was facing the most ferocious Luftwaffe opposition of the war. The F variant was the Fort used to develop the technique of daylight precision bombing.

The heart of AAF bombing doctrine was self-defense of the mission through tight-formation flying and concentrated firepower from powered turrets and flexible guns. General Arnold and his prewar staff were the first to admit their lack of interest in long range escort fighters was a near fatal mistake. Luftwaffe pilots and flak gunners proved far more tenacious than anyone had imagined. Fortunately the B-17, which bore the brunt of the effort, was easy to fly, forgiving, rugged, and if necessary, able to belly land.

In September 1943 the AAF reached the peak of its B-17 inventory with 6,043, most serving in thirty-three groups overseas, compared to over 8,000 B-24 Liberators in forty-five and a half groups. The two aircraft had a continual rivalry between their crews, particularly when they served in the same theater.

Crews of Forts and Libs became zealous about the strong points of their particular aircraft, something quite normal in the face of fierce enemy opposition. B-24 crews claimed, and rightly so, their bomber could fly faster and carry more bombs farther than the B-17. Fortress crews claimed, quite properly, their bomber could take more battle damage and survive a belly landing better than the Liberator. The heated arguments were not helped a bit by the lopsided publicity given the B-17. Liberator crews were always complaining they never got the press they deserved, particularly since more B-24s (18,432, thanks to Henry Ford) were built than any single American aircraft in history, quite a record for a heavy bomber.

After the Schweinfurt raid of 14 October 1943, when sixty bombers failed to come home out of 229, the Eighth Air Force had to cease deep penetration missions until P-47s, P-38s, and P-51s could escort them all the way to the target and back. Had it not been for these fighters and their pilots, the AAF Strategic Bombing Offensive would have failed. Fortunately, strategic bombing survived due to tenacious fighter pilots and the dedication of the American worker who funneled thousands upon thousands (eventually a total of 299,293) of aircraft into the combat zones. The Eighth Air Force expanded to the point of flying from England in three air divisions with twenty-six bomb groups.

A box of 401st Squadron, 91st Bomb Group B-17Fs, escorted by P-47s, climb out over England in early 1943. The 91st, based at Bassingbourn, was one of the pioneer Eighth Air Force heavy bomb groups and the first to attack a target in the Ruhr-Hamm area on 4 March 1943. Unfortunately those Thunderbolts would never be able to escort the bombers far enough to protect them deep in enemy territory. *USAF*

⭐ MEDITERRANEAN FORTRESS ⭐

Forts flying with the 2nd, 97th, 99th, and 301st Bomb Groups out of North Africa carried the war deep into Axis held territory by bombing targets in Greece, Austria, Yugoslavia, and southern France. They later moved on to Italy to hit Germany itself. When the Fifteenth Air Force was formed in Italy in late 1943, the Twelfth's four B-17 groups transferred over and with another two groups, made up the total Fortress complement. Now the AAF could hit Germany with B-17s and B-24s from both west and south. This forced production czar Albert Speer to disperse Germany's industries and move as much of them underground as possible.

✪ ETERNAL FORTRESS ✪

In spite of the controversy over the effectiveness of strategic bombardment—which rages to this day—the effort was a vital component to the Allied victory, particularly when viewed through German eyes. After the war Speer remarked, "The American [bomber] attacks, which followed a definite system of assault on industrial targets, were by far the most dangerous. It was, in fact, these attacks which caused the breakdown of the German armaments industry. The attacks on the chemical industry would have sufficed, without the impact of purely military events, to render Germany defenseless."

The final Flying Fortress model, the B-17G, began to arrive in England in September 1943. By the spring of 1944, it was the version most responsible for carrying the war to Germany from both England and Italy. The B-17G was easily recognized by the addition of a chin turret below the nose. The Eighth Air Force had a peak strength of 2,370 B-17Gs by March 1945.

With V-E Day the Flying Fortress became useless as a weapon of war. In the hot American southwest summer of 1946,

Outdoor maintenance was the rule around the globe, particularly in the Mediterreanean and the Pacific. Seargent Guy Kellog on the work stand, Pfc. George Meterhott (lying down on No. 4 cowling), and Pfc. Henry Moeller (on No. 3 cowling) get their B-17G ready near Foggia, Italy, 1944. If the weather was bad the work still had to be done, even in freezing cold or driving rain. Who ever said war was fun? *USAF*

1,832 B-17s stretched across the Arizona desert at Kingman Army Air Base awaiting the scrapper's torch. A dim memory for a nation obsessed with getting back to peacetime, raising families, and enjoying a world in which there would never be war again. A few escaped to become rescue patrol aircraft for the US Coast Guard, others stayed in the new US Air Force as VIP or research aircraft. The US Navy even kept a few PB-1Ws carrying large radars for airborne search and patrol against enemy fleets and submarines. The Navy used their Forts until they were replaced with purpose-built radar search aircraft like the Grumman S-1 Tracker.

Paul Mantz, the famous Hollywood stunt pilot, saved a few for movie work, most famous for appearing in *Twelve O'clock High*. Several Fortresses endured to become borate chemical forest-fire bombers, dangerous work among horrible down drafts which took almost as heavy a toll as combat. Due to their excellent load carrying capability and large wing (excellent lift), these B-17s "bombed" fire-endangered forests until the early 1980s when they were, at last, retired and auctioned off to collectors as rare historic artifacts.

From 1942 to 1945 B-17s dropped 640,036 tons of bombs on European targets compared to 452,508 tons from B-24s. Pilots commented it flew about like a Piper Cub with the same forgiving characteristics. Frank Prendergast, pilot of the 388th Bomb Group's Fort *Jamaica Ginger*

recalled, "The B-17 always seemed to handle like a light plane on takeoff and landing. It had no undesirable characteristics." Eighth Air Force technical officer Cass Hough "loved to fly the Fortress—it was such a big bird; it always seemed to me to be very responsive and to have a real soul."

The darling of the AAF's public relations effort, the Flying Fortress will forever be established in the American mind as the aircraft that brought the war to the enemy.

Left, athe crew of this 97th Bomb Group B-17G has just arrived at their hardstand (no cement here!) at Amendola, Italy. The mud on the tires and muffler of this jeep say it all...Italy was known for its gumbo mud almost all year round. The 97th was another of the Fifteenth Air Force's pioneer Fortress groups, having flown its first combat missions from England with the Eighth in 1942 before being sent to North Africa that November. *USAF*

Above, a veteran B-17F, stripped of its armament, sits at Mt. Farm, England with some of its welcome Little Friends...Dave Schilling's 56th Fighter Group P-47D and two 339th Fighter Group P-51s. These faster Forts roamed England taking the brass to meetings or visits to airfields under their command.
Robert Astrella

Above, a new 388th Bomb Group replacement B-17G from Knettishall, without a single mission yet to its credit, visits Mt. Farm, England, late summer 1944.
Robert Astrella

Right, Major James McPartlin, pilot of the 91st Bomb Group's *General "Ike"*, gets a dunking at Bassingbourn after flying his last mission. The nose art was typical of Sgt. Tony Starcer's attention to detail, the reason he ended up painting most of the aircraft in the group. By the time a crew had finished their tour they were either close knit or at odds...there was no in-between. Rarely did an entire crew start and finish together either due to illness, transfers, and death in combat. *USAF*

Above, though a study in contrasts, this 91st Bomb Group B-17G and L-4 Grasshopper at Bassingbourn, England, were not that different, according to Fort pilots. The most common compliment was how easy a B-17 was to fly. It landed just like a great big Piper Cub. It took off and landed three points effortlessly, even under a full load. *USAF*

Left, attached to the 379th Bomb Group at Kimbolton, *The Wish Bone* flew until it was worn out and set aside, as is evident from the patchwork olive drab paint. After putting in 88 missions, the B-17G was used to train new crews in operational procedures, then finally pushed aside. The older Forts were known for their sloppy controls (stretched cables) and worn equipment. Many went through several complete engine changes. *Arnold N. Delmonico*

Above, *The Bad Penny* lived up to her name and always came back to her 96th Bomb Group base at Snetterton Heath, even through the very dark days of 1943 when the Eighth Air Force was getting hammered by the Luftwaffe. This was quite remarkable considering most 96th B-17Fs never survived their combat tours. Before being scrapped, she was given to the 3rd Air Division to transition B-24 pilots into the B-17.
Arnold N. Delmonico

Left, the 490th Bomb Group at Eye was known for some of the more daring nose art in the Eighth Air Force, as *£5 with Breakfast* clearly displays. The name reflected the offer usually made by the more sophisticated London prostitutes. No doubt the airplane got quite a bit of attention wherever it showed up.
Arnold N. Delmonico

Left, A 94th Bomb Group, 331st Squadron B-17G just after lift-off from Bury St. Edmunds, England, spring 1945. The acceptable take-off procedure, according to the Pilot's Handbook, was to keep the tail low with the tailwheel just off the ground and let the aircraft fly off in climbing attitude at the ideal angle of attack. This usually resulted in a very smooth take-off and got the Fort off as short as possible. Many pilots preferred to push the wheel forward and get the tail level to accelerate so there were arguments between the two schools of thought.
Robert Astrella

Above, B-17Gs of the 381st Bomb Group climb out toward Europe in the fall of 1944 carrying the colorful red markings of the 1st Combat Bomb Wing. At this point in the war, the Eighth Air Force had instituted a policy of allowing each bomb wing within the three air divisions to paint their aircraft with unique paint schemes. This allowed groups and wings to form up faster, and it also boosted morale. No one twenty years old wanted to fly in a drab airplane.
USAF

Above, a pair of B-17Gs from the 306th Bomb Group at Thurliegh head out over England in early May 1945. The group's yellow tail band went through the triangle H while the squadron color, in this case the 367th's red, was painted on the tip of the vertical tail. The great silver fleets of 1945 were the ultimate symbol of victory, roaming Germany at will under thick fighter cover.
Ben Marcilonis via Roger Freeman

Left, with engines coming up to full power, a 490th Bomb Group B-17G begins its take-off roll at Eye, England, Station 134. In spite of slow initial acceleration, particularly with a full load, the Fortress was known for its ability to get airborne with just about any load thanks to its very high-lift wing. That same wing gave it better high altitude performance than the B-24. Even when pushed beyond her limits, the B-17 usually came through.
Arnold N. Delmonico

Above, B-17Fs heading for Germany in 1943, the roughest year of the war for the Eighth Air Force. In spite of some of the tightest formation flying ever performed, it was not enough to protect bombers from skilled, battle-hardened German fighter pilots. Even so, Luftwaffe crews found it rough-going trying to fly through these boxes of bombers with a hail of bullets crashing into their aircraft every time they came through. Both sides were not willing to give an inch.
USAF via Stan Piet

Right, the 457th Bomb Group lets go of its 1,000 pounders over Germany on 10 April 1945 with Sky Marker smoke still hanging in the air to the left. With less than a month to go before the war ended, enemy skies were still dangerous. Only a short time later the group was attacked by Me 262 jet fighters, which downed two of the unit's Forts as well as others of the nineteen bombers lost that day. Ironically the mission had been against suspected jet airfields.
Arthur Fitch

Left, 1st Lt. Willis H. Kennedy, Jr., pilot of this 91st Bomb Group Fort at Bassingbourn, poses with the weary look of experience, 1945. By today's standards, flying equipment was simple and in many ways inadequate for war at 30,000 feet where the air was -60 degrees F. The leading cause of casualties during the bomber offensive was not fighters, flak, or even accidents...it was frostbite. Men would often come back with black hands or feet, at times losing their toes and fingers.
National Archives

Above, climbing out of Great Ashfield for Germany, a 385th Bomb Group B-17G races the rising sun in late 1944. Getting up at "oh dark thirty" for a mission was never easy, particularly if take-off time was before or just after sunrise. American planners were very smart in limiting missions to, at first 25, then later 35, rather than keeping crews in combat until they were either maimed or killed. It was rough enough as it was.
Clark B. Rollins, Jr.

Above, Major Byron Trent, commander of the 94th Bomb Group's 333rd Squadron, in front of his squadron orderly room at Bury St. Edmunds. These half-concrete, half-corrugated tin Nissen Huts—easy to build and hard to heat—were the mainstay of Eighth Air Force operations. Without them the war would have been much tougher, particularly in those damp, cold English winters.
Byron E. Trent

Left, one of the few areas under camouflage at a bomber base...the bomb dump at Bury St. Edmunds, home of the 94th Bomb Group, 1945. Right up until the end of the war, German raiders would sneak into England to bomb targets of opportunity so the precaution was well taken...the last thing anyone needed was the bomb dumb to go up.
Byron E. Trent

The Disney rocket bomb was one of those Buck Rogers ideas British scientists were encouraged to try. Major Byron Trent stands next to the second test rocket at Bury St. Edmunds, spring 1945. The 94th Bomb Group was to test the 14 foot long, 4,500 pound Disney's ability to penetrate German reinforced concrete structures when launched from the external bomb rack of a B-17. The first combat mission with the 2,400 foot-per-second rocket failed when it wouldn't release, and the war ended before another one could be launched. Though not guided, the weapon was a look at the future.

Byron E. Trent

Above, *Skippy*, an old 306th Bomb Group veteran B-17G with a shiney new tail, flies over England with another 367th Squadron Fort in early May 1945. Rarely did a B-17 last this long (she started flying combat in February 1944 and passed 100 missions), but even after being heavily damaged she kept flying.
Ben Marcilonis via Roger Freeman

Right, late in the war *Short Arm*, 833rd Squadron, 486th Bomb Group, flies over England when everything was just about over. The 1945 colors of Eighth Air Force bomber and fighter outfits were the most colorful applied to any large organization of combat aircraft. CO Jimmy Doolittle had a real flair for understanding what motivated combat aircrew...paint was just about the cheapest form of morale one could buy.
Alexander C. Sloan

Next page, May 1945...the war is over, and *Lassie Come Home* has lived up to her name for the last time at her 367th Squadron, 306th Bomb Group base of Thurleigh. Damaged and patched several times, the Fort's OD replacement rudder has even been patched again. Most of these veterans would survive only to be scrapped.
Ben Marcilonis via Roger Freeman

Post-mission refueling at Knettishall, 26 August 1944... *Miss Fortune*, 561st Squadron, 388th Bomb Group had just led the high squadron to Brest and back. Ground crews wasted little time in getting their aircraft back in operational condition...the faster it was over with, the faster they could get some much needed rest before getting up in the very early hours of the morning to preflight and warm up the aircraft. Outdoor maintenance in England was never much fun unless the day was like ths one.
Mark Brown/USAFA

A box of three 381st Bomb Group B-17Gs begins to close on the box ahead as the group forms up over England. There was no sense in flying real tight formation until over the Channel and heading into enemy territory. Time stretched out long enough as it was when jockeying yoke and throttles for hours at a time.
USAF

A 95th Bomb Group Fort climbs out of Horham, August 1944. When English weather was good, it was spectacular, with crystal clear skies, excellent visibility, and pleasant temperatures.
Albert J. Keeler

Next page left, the bombardier of 95th Bomb Group B-17G *Full House*, 1st Lt. Foster Sherwood had his share of adventures, many on the ground chasing girls. After surviving thirty-five missions as a part of George Dancisin's crew, he was killed in a postwar airplane crash. The bombardier's job was often the toughest to do since he had to make split second decisions about dropping the bombs when weather was marginal...he also was one of the most vulnerable crew members, sitting in the front of the Plexiglas nose with no armor between him and attacking fighters.
Albert J. Keeler

Next page right, most crews had a budding artist...on *Full House* in the 95th Bomb Group at Horham it was tail gunner S/Sgt. Larry Stevens who painted the jackets in George Dancisin's crew. Every gunner on a B-17 was vulnerable, but none were more isolated than the tail gunner, at the very end of the aircraft on the other side of the tail wheel.
Albert J. Keeler

Just back from a mission, the 100th Bomb Group crew of *Lady Geraldine* slowly gather their parachutes and personal equipment before heading to debriefing at Thorpe Abbots. Missions which lasted upwards of eight hours were so exhausting there was little energy left to talk about them.

Debriefing officers were often the brunt of the anger and frustration built up in combat, yet post mission information was crucial to planning the next series of deep penetrations. *Mark Brown/USAFA*

Station defense at Thorpe Abbots, home of the 100th Bomb Group, consisted of several water cooled machine gun pits, not that much could be done against a low-flying German raider which came and went in seconds. *Mark Brown/USAFA*

The 447th Bomb Group's *Blond Bomber II* saw her share of combat flying with the 710th Squadron out of Rattlesden. The famous Vargas one-armed girl appeared on numerous bombers since her first appearance in Esquire. *Mark Brown/USAFA*

Ole Timer lived up to its name, flying its first series of missions with the 391st Squadron, 34th Bomb Group out of Mendlesham, then finishing its tour with the 490th Group at Eye, still carrying the 34th's markings for a time. *Mark Brown/USAFA*

A line of TB-17G drones and drone controllers of the 509th Composite Group, 58th Bomb Wing, await their fate at Eniwetok Island. Four drones were to be flown through the mushroom clouds created during Operation Crossroads, the Bikini atomic bomb test of 1 July, 1946. At the dawn of the atomic age the Fort was to withstand the ultimate weapon.
USAF

Above, the colorful markings of the AAF's fledgling All Weather Flying Center would make any B-17 stand out. Flying from Clinton County AAF, Ohio, from March 1946 to October 1949, then Wright-Patterson AFB, the unit, using a variety of aircraft, developed procedures and equipment for all-weather flying, an important capability for line squadrons. *Joe Voellmeck via Frederick A. Johnsen*

Left, a U.S. Coast Guard PB-1G on the line at Logan Field, Massachusetts, May 1955. Operating as long-range air-sea rescue patrol aircraft, the last of the Forts was withdrawn from service in April 1959. They could search visually and with radar while some carried aerial mapping cameras in the ball-turret position. *P. Paulsen via David W. Menard*

Previous page, one of Fifth Air Force's VB-17s at Nellis AFB, Nevada, in the late 1940s is shined and polished to suit any general. The obsolete bomber, with so much room, became an ideal VIP transport after the war. This was particularly the case with non-current generals wanting to fly their own airplanes...the Fort was so easy to fly almost anyone could handle it, particularly with a good co-pilot in the other seat. *Richard B. Keener*

INDEX